TOILETRIVIA

SPORTS

The only trivia book that caters to your everyday bathroom needs

by Jeremy Klaff & Harry Klaff

This book might contain product names, trademarks, or registered trademarks. All trademarks in this book are property of their respective owners. If used, they are for non-biased use, and we do not encourage or discourage use of said product or service. Any term suspected of being a trademark will be properly capitalized.

Cover art by Stephanie Strack

About the Authors

Harry Klaff covered the NHL for *The Hockey News* and *Hockey Pictorial*, and reported for both the Associated Press and United Press International. He has written three books, *All Time Greatest Super Bowl*, *All Time Greatest Stanley Cup*, and *Computer Literacy and Use*.

Today, he is a retired Social Studies teacher from Brooklyn. Because he never went on a date in his adolescence, Harry had plenty of time to research useless facts and figures on everything ranging from history to pop culture. Moonlighting as a hockey scoreboard operator and baseball beer vendor, Harry had ample time to collect data.

Yet somehow, he got married. In 1977, Jeremy was born. Rather than being raised on a steady diet of carrots and peas, baby Jeremy was forced to learn facts from textbooks. His first word was "Uzbekistan." Throughout his childhood, Jeremy had a hard time making friends. When other kids wanted to play baseball, he wanted to instruct them about Henry VIII's six wives. After a failed career as a standup comic and broadcaster, in 2000 Jeremy fittingly became a Social Studies teacher. Today he brings trivia to the next generation.

Collect All Toiletrivia Titles

US History

World History

Pop Culture

Sports

Baseball

Music

and more!

Get the full list of titles at
www.toiletrivia.com

Acknowledgements

We at Toiletrivia would like to thank all of the people who made this possible.

- The ancient cities of Harappa and Mohenjo Daro for engineering advances in plumbing.

- Sir John Harrington for inventing the modern flush toilet.

- Seth Wheeler for his patent of perforated toilet paper.

- Jeffrey Gunderson for inventing the plunger.

We would like to thank our families for suffering through nights of endless trivia.

We would also like to thank the friendly commuters at the Grand Central Station restroom facility for field testing these editions.

Introduction

Here at *Toiletrivia* we do extensive research on what you, the bathroom user, wish to see in your reading material. Sure, there are plenty of fine books out there to pass the time, but none of them cater to your competitive needs. That's why *Toiletrivia* is here to provide captivating trivia that allows you to interact with fellow bathroom users.

Each chapter allows you to keep score so you can evaluate your progress if you choose to go through the book multiple times. Or, you may wish to leave the book behind for others to play and keep score against you. Perhaps you just want to make it look like you are a genius, and leave a perfect scorecard for all to see. We hope you leave one in every bathroom of the house.

The rules of *Toiletrivia* are simple. Each chapter has 30 questions divided into three sections…One Roll, Two Rolls, or Three Rolls. The One Rolls are easiest and worth one point. Two Rolls are a bit harder and are worth two points. And of course, Three Rolls are the hardest, and are worth three points. You will tabulate your progress on the scorecard near the end of the book.

The questions we have selected are meant for dinner conversation, or impressing people you want to date. With few exceptions, our queries are geared for the uncomfortable situations that life throws at you, like when you have nothing in common with someone, and need to offer some clever banter. We hope that the facts you learn in the restroom make it easier to meet your future in-laws, or deal with that hairdresser who just won't stop talking to you.

Remember, *Toiletrivia* is a game. No joysticks, no computer keyboards…just you, your toilet, and a pen; the way nature intended it. So good luck. We hope you are triumphant.

DIRECTIONS

Each set of questions has an answer sheet opposite it. Write your answers in the first available column to the right. When you are done with a set of 10 questions, *fold* your answer column underneath so the next restroom user doesn't see your answers. *Special note to restroom users 2 and 3: No cheating! And the previous person's answers might be wrong!*

Then check your responses with the answer key in the back of the book. Mark your right answers with a check, and your wrong answers with an "x." Then go to the scorecard on pages 98-100 and tabulate your results. These totals will be the standard for other users to compare.

Be sure to look online for other Toiletrivia titles
Visit us at www.toiletrivia.com

Table of Contents

Football 8

Baseball 14

Basketball 20

Hockey 26

Golf & Tennis 32

Rules 38

Racing—All Kinds 44

Personalities 50

Famous Firsts 56

Everything & Anything 62

Football Answers 68

Baseball Answers 71

Basketball Answers 74

Hockey Answers 77

Golf & Tennis Answers 80

Rules Answers 83

Racing—All Kinds Answers 86

Personalities Answers 89

Famous Firsts Answers 92

Everything & Anything Answers 95

Scorecards 98

Football

One Roll

Flip to pg. 68 for answers

1. What quarterback has thrown for the most yards in NFL history? He also holds the record for the most retirements.

2. Which Buffalo Bills kicker went "wide right" as time expired in Super Bowl XXV?

3. What southpaw was Joe Montana's backup in the late 1980s? He eventually went on to championship glory as well.

4. What kitchen appliance was the nickname for a Bears defensive lineman who was used as an offensive tool in short distance situations?

5. What "primetime" Hall of Famer played in 641 Major League Baseball games?

6. Joined by former players such as Frank Gifford and Don Meredith, he was an announcer on *Monday Night Football*. You might also know this iconic voice from his coverage and interaction with Muhammad Ali.

7. Who was known as "The Galloping Ghost"?

8. What Lions running back and athletic magician retired at age 31, about 1,500 yards short of breaking Walter Payton's all-time rushing record?

9. At the age of 23, what player became the youngest quarterback to win a Super Bowl?

10. Where is the Pro Football Hall of Fame located?

Answer Sheet   Answer Sheet   Answer Sheet

<table>
<tr><td>Football
1 Roll</td><td>Football
1 Roll</td><td>Football
1 Roll</td></tr>
<tr><td>Name_____</td><td>Name_____</td><td>Name_____</td></tr>
</table>

1.	1.	1.
2.	2.	2.
3.	3.	3.
4.	4.	4.
5.	5.	5.
6.	6.	6.
7.	7.	7.
8.	8.	8.
9.	9.	9.
10.	10.	10.

After you have filled out the sheet, fold your column underneath along the dashed line so the next restroom user won't see your answers. *The first player uses the far right column.*

Notes: *Notes:*   *Notes:*

Football

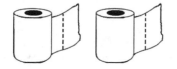

Two Rolls

Flip to pg. 69 for answers

1. Peyton and Eli's dad, Archie, was a quarterback too. Name one of the three teams he played for.

2. What Heisman Trophy winner did Tom Landry call, "possibly the best combination of a passer, an athlete, and a leader to ever play in the NFL"?

3. In 1958, who played whom in "The Greatest Game Ever Played"?

4. For those watching at home, what children's TV-movie interrupted the closing moments of a Jets-Raiders game in 1968?

5. Name the Dallas Cowboys defensive tackle who made two infamous blunders. First, he botched picking up a missed field goal that ultimately led to a loss on Thanksgiving. Second, while showboating a sure touchdown in Super Bowl XXVII, he was blind-sided by Don Beebe, and had the ball knocked out of his hand resulting in a touchback.

6. On December 31, 1988 the Bears beat the Eagles 20-12. The only problem was, no one could see it! Why?

7. What usually high-ranked college team from the Mountain West Conference plays on blue turf?

8. This great 1950s-1960s fullback still holds the Cleveland Browns record of 1,863 rushing yards in one season. He also appeared on the Silver Screen in *The Dirty Dozen*.

9. 1969 was the first time an AFL team won the Super Bowl. Who won and who lost? We *guarantee* that you know the answer.

10. What quarterback has the most passing yards with no Super Bowl ring?

Answer Sheet

Football
2 Rolls

Name_____

1.
2.
3.
4.
5.
6.
7.
8.
9.
10.

Answer Sheet

Football
2 Rolls

Name_____

1.
2.
3.
4.
5.
6.
7.
8.
9.
10.

Answer Sheet

Football
2 Rolls

Name_____

1.
2.
3.
4.
5.
6.
7.
8.
9.
10.

After you have filled out the sheet, fold your column underneath along the dashed line so the next restroom user won't see your answers. *The first player uses the far right column.*

Notes:

Notes:

Notes:

Football

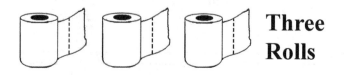

Three Rolls

Flip to pg. 70 for answers

1. Who scored the winning touchdown in the 1978 "Miracle at the Meadowlands"?

2. In 2007, Chargers defensive back Antonio Cromartie set an NFL record by running 109+ yards for a touchdown. How did he get the ball?

3. Prior to 1971, where did the Chicago Bears play their home games?

4. What was the league that existed between 1946 and 1949, and included the San Francisco 49ers and the Cleveland Browns?

5. Once known as one of Fordham University's Seven Blocks of Granite, his philosophy was that winning was the only thing.

6. What team posted the most one-sided victory in NFL history?

7. From goal line to goal line, how long is the field in the Canadian Football League?

8. Name one of the two men who have won a Super Bowl as a player, assistant coach, and a head coach.

9. The Arizona Cardinals have played in two other cities. What are they?

10. Within 10 points, what was the highest score ever put up by one team in a collegiate or professional football game?

Answer Sheet

Football
3 Rolls

Name_____

1.	
2.	
3.	
4.	
5.	
6.	
7.	
8.	
9.	
10.	

Answer Sheet

Football
3 Rolls

Name_____

1.	
2.	
3.	
4.	
5.	
6.	
7.	
8.	
9.	
10.	

Answer Sheet

Football
3 Rolls

Name_____

1.	
2.	
3.	
4.	
5.	
6.	
7.	
8.	
9.	
10.	

After you have filled out the sheet, fold your column underneath along the dashed line so the next restroom user won't see your answers. *The first player uses the far right column.*

Notes:

Notes:

Notes:

Baseball

One Roll

Flip to pg. 71 for answers

1. What did Pete Rose do on September 11, 1985 that gave him a prime spot in the record books?

2. Who holds the record of hitting in 56 consecutive games?

3. This team and the New York Mets were National League expansion teams in 1962. The team's nickname was "shot down" a few years later.

4. Which pitcher has the most career strikeouts?

5. What ballpark features "The Pesky Pole"?

6. Who was known as "The Iron Horse," or "Larrupin' Lou"?

7. This team has not won a World Series since 1908.

8. Pine tar or no pine tar, he is the only player elected to the Hall of Fame as a member of the Kansas City Royals.

9. In 2004 and 2005, two clubs ended nearly 90 years of World Series drought. Name both.

10. On a scorecard, a player is out, 4-3. What does that mean?

Answer Sheet   Answer Sheet   Answer Sheet

Baseball
1 Roll

Baseball
1 Roll

Baseball
1 Roll

Name_____   Name_____   Name_____

1.	1.	1.
2.	2.	2.
3.	3.	3.
4.	4.	4.
5.	5.	5.
6.	6.	6.
7.	7.	7.
8.	8.	8.
9.	9.	9.
10.	10.	10.

After you have filled out the sheet, fold your column underneath along the dashed line so the next restroom user won't see your answers. *The first player uses the far right column.*

Notes: *Notes:*   *Notes:*

Baseball

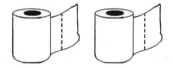 **Two Rolls**

Flip to pg. 72 for answers

1. This American League manager was kicked out of almost 100 games, including Game Four of the 1969 World Series.

2. What is Chipper Jones' real first name?

3. Paul McCartney joined Billy Joel for the final concert at this ballpark on July 19, 2008.

4. What was Hall of Fame pitcher George Waddell better known as? It was a common baseball nickname given to anyone who came from "the sticks." 1950s Dodgers catcher Walker had the same one.

5. What Astro set a postseason record in 2004 by clubbing home runs in five consecutive games?

6. This knuckleballer finished with 3,342 strikeouts. He was still baffling hitters until he retired in 1988.

7. With a mark of .344, this slugger had the highest lifetime batting average for someone playing as late as the 1960s.

8. According to the Baseball Hall of Fame, this Negro League catcher hit almost 800 home runs.

9. Who is the only man to win the MVP Award in each league? He's also the only person to ever hit a home run completely out of old Baltimore Memorial Stadium.

10. When Jackie Robinson's Number 42 was retired throughout baseball in 1997, players who were currently wearing those digits were allowed to retain them. Who is the last player to hold onto Number 42?

Answer Sheet	Answer Sheet	Answer Sheet
Baseball **2 Rolls**	**Baseball** **2 Rolls**	**Baseball** **2 Rolls**
Name_____	Name_____	Name_____
1.	1.	1.
2.	2.	2.
3.	3.	3.
4.	4.	4.
5.	5.	5.
6.	6.	6.
7.	7.	7.
8.	8.	8.
9.	9.	9.
10.	10.	10.

After you have filled out the sheet, fold your column underneath along the dashed line so the next restroom user won't see your answers. *The first player uses the far right column.*

Notes: *Notes:*   *Notes:*

Baseball

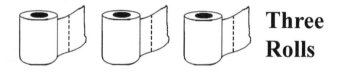

Three Rolls

Flip to pg. 73 for answers

1. This classic ballpark's right field wall was only 258 feet from home plate, but dead center was 483 feet.

2. Who was the first Japanese pitcher to hurl a no-hitter in the Major Leagues?

3. In 2009, this White Sox hurler became the sixth pitcher in history to record both a perfect game and a no-hitter in a career. He also set a record by retiring 45 consecutive hitters over three games.

4. Who hit the most home runs in the 1950s?

5. This minor league ballpark was also the home of the AFL-NFL Buffalo Bills from 1960-1972. Many scenes in *The Natural* were filmed there.

6. Name the umpire whose blown call in Game 6 at first base helped the Kansas City Royals beat the St. Louis Cardinals in the 1985 World Series?

7. Three players have appeared in a record 24 All-Star Games. Name two of them.

8. This guy nicknamed "Sparky" was a relief pitcher for a bunch of teams in the 1960s-1970s, but played mostly for the Red Sox and Yankees.

9. A lefty, this Brooklyn native finished with 424 career saves, mostly with his hometown New York Mets.

10. This all-around athlete played baseball for the Dodgers and Cubs (and basketball for the Boston Celtics), but he is remembered most for being TV's *The Rifleman*.

Answer Sheet | # Answer Sheet | # Answer Sheet

| Baseball
3 Rolls | Baseball
3 Rolls | Baseball
3 Rolls |

Name_____ Name_____ Name_____

1.	1.	1.
2.	2.	2.
3.	3.	3.
4.	4.	4.
5.	5.	5.
6.	6.	6.
7.	7.	7.
8.	8.	8.
9.	9.	9.
10.	10.	10.

After you have filled out the sheet, fold your column underneath along the dashed line so the next restroom user won't see your answers. *The first player uses the far right column.*

Notes: | *Notes:* | *Notes:*

19

Basketball

One Roll

Flip to pg. 74 for answers

1. The only player to score 100 points in an NBA game, he also claimed to have had 10,000 girlfriends.

2. This legendary coach of the Boston Celtics won 9 NBA Championships, and was an expert on Chinese food. When he lit his cigar, you knew the game was in the bag.

3. What was the nickname given to the US Men's Basketball Team at the 1992 Summer Games in Barcelona?

4. What team has won the most NCAA Division I Men's Basketball Championships?

5. What member of the "Fab Five" University of Michigan team called a time-out with 11 seconds to go in the 1993 NCAA Division I Men's Basketball Championship Game? Unfortunately, the team was out of time-outs, and a technical foul was called.

6. What team has won the most NBA Championships, and boasts the most retired numbers?

7. What is Dr. J's real name?

8. What college basketball team set a record in 2010 by winning their 89th straight game?

9. What was Kareem Abdul-Jabbar's name at birth?

10. Michael Jordan wore two numbers with the Chicago Bulls. Name them.

Answer Sheet   Answer Sheet   Answer Sheet

Basketball   Basketball   Basketball
1 Roll   1 Roll   1 Roll

Name_____   Name_____   Name_____

1.	1.	1.
2.	2.	2.
3.	3.	3.
4.	4.	4.
5.	5.	5.
6.	6.	6.
7.	7.	7.
8.	8.	8.
9.	9.	9.
10.	10.	10.

After you have filled out the sheet, fold your column underneath along the dashed line so the next restroom user won't see your answers. *The first player uses the far right column.*

Notes: *Notes:*   *Notes:*

Basketball

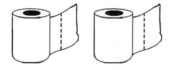

Two Rolls

Flip to pg. 75 for answers

1. This dazzling showman is the NCAA Division I all-time career-leading scorer.

2. What New York Knicks guard dunked over Horace Grant and Michael Jordan in the 1993 NBA Playoffs?

3. Who "stole the ball," after an inbound pass from 76er Hal Greer to clinch the Eastern Conference Championship for the Celtics in 1965?

4. From 2000-2010, three players won the NBA Most Valuable Player Award twice. Can you name two of them?

5. What college did Larry Bird play for?

6. What team do the Harlem Globetrotters continually defeat?

7. Known as "Mr. Basketball," this star of the 1940s and early 1950s was so adept at blocking shots that the foul lane had to be widened.

8. Loved by his fans and despised by his opponents, this Detroit Pistons center went on to coach the Detroit Shock to WNBA Championships in 2003, 2006, and 2008.

9. Name four of the six NBA teams that Shaquille O'Neal played for.

10. Phil Jackson has coached the most NBA champions with 11. What team did he spend most of his playing career with?

Answer Sheet | # Answer Sheet | # Answer Sheet

Basketball
2 Rolls

Basketball
2 Rolls

Basketball
2 Rolls

Name_____ Name_____ Name_____

1.	1.	1.
2.	2.	2.
3.	3.	3.
4.	4.	4.
5.	5.	5.
6.	6.	6.
7.	7.	7.
8.	8.	8.
9.	9.	9.
10.	10.	10.

After you have filled out the sheet, fold your column underneath along the dashed line so the next restroom user won't see your answers. *The first player uses the far right column.*

Notes: *Notes:*   *Notes:*

Basketball

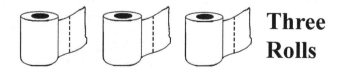

Three Rolls

Flip to pg. 76 for answers

1. Who is the only NBA player to average a triple-double for an entire season?

2. In 1987, the Washington Bullets had both the shortest and tallest players in NBA history on their team. Who were they?

3. In 1966, what college was the first to start an all African American line-up in an NCAA Division I Men's Basketball Championship Game? The team defeated Kentucky, and would be the subject of the 2006 film *Glory Road*.

4. Who was the MVP of the first four WNBA Finals?

5. They weren't players, but New York's John Condon and Philadelphia's Dave Zinkoff were well known to fans from the 1940s and beyond. What were they famous for?

6. What team from Onondaga County in New York moved to Philadelphia in 1963 to become the 76ers?

7. This New York City-based school won the NCAA Division I Men's Basketball Championship in 1950, but was sadly involved in a point-shaving scandal shortly thereafter.

8. What college, located in Worcester, Massachusetts, did Bob Cousy help lead to the NCAA Men's Basketball Championship in 1947?

9. The first NBA Champions in 1946-47 are still around. But they moved from an eastern city to one out west in 1962.

10. The first President of the NBA (and its predecessor, the BAA) was a Russian immigrant. Today the league's Most Valuable Player trophy is named for him.

Answer Sheet   Answer Sheet   Answer Sheet

<table>
<tr><td>Basketball
3 Rolls</td><td>Basketball
3 Rolls</td><td>Basketball
3 Rolls</td></tr>
</table>

Name_____   Name_____   Name_____

1.	1.	1.
2.	2.	2.
3.	3.	3.
4.	4.	4.
5.	5.	5.
6.	6.	6.
7.	7.	7.
8.	8.	8.
9.	9.	9.
10.	10.	10.

After you have filled out the sheet, fold your column underneath along the dashed line so the next restroom user won't see your answers. ***The first player uses the far right column.***

Notes: *Notes:*   *Notes:*

Hockey

One Roll

Flip to pg. 77 for answers

1. What team has won the most Stanley Cups?

2. Name four current franchises that made up the "Original Six" NHL teams.

3. What number was Wayne Gretzky?

4. What have fans in Detroit been known to throw on the ice to spark offense?

5. Where is the NHL Hall of Fame located?

6. What is the area between the two blue lines called?

7. How many minutes in the penalty box does one get for a major penalty?

8. What television network debuted a glowing puck in its coverage of games in the 1990s?

9. Name one of the father and son pair that combined for almost 1,400 goals in their careers. You may know them better as "The Golden Jet," and "The Golden Brett."

10. What goalie has the most games played, wins, and shutouts in NHL history? He has spent his entire career with the same team.

Answer Sheet

Hockey
1 Roll

Name_____

1.
2.
3.
4.
5.
6.
7.
8.
9.
10.

Answer Sheet

Hockey
1 Roll

Name_____

1.
2.
3.
4.
5.
6.
7.
8.
9.
10.

Answer Sheet

Hockey
1 Roll

Name_____

1.
2.
3.
4.
5.
6.
7.
8.
9.
10.

After you have filled out the sheet, fold your column underneath along the dashed line so the next restroom user won't see your answers. *The first player uses the far right column.*

Notes:

Notes:

Notes:

Hockey

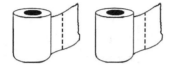 **Two Rolls**

Flip to pg. 78 for answers

1. What was the legendary home of the Montreal Canadiens from 1926-1996?

2. Why was there no Stanley Cup winner in 1919? The answer involves a disease.

3. Who was the Soviet Union's stellar goaltender when they faced Canada's NHL stars in 1972? In 1980, he was pulled in the "Miracle on Ice" game.

4. Name the famous Montreal Canadiens broadcaster who used colorful phrases such as "scintillating save" and "cannonading drive."

5. What was the first US-based team in the NHL?

6. Who held the record for most career goals until Wayne Gretzky came along?

7. This New York Islanders great started his career with nine straight seasons scoring 50+ goals.

8. What position wins the Vezina Trophy?

9. On March 23, 1952, how many goals did Chicago's Bill Mosienko score in 21 seconds?

10. The US won the Gold Medal at the winter games in 1960, twenty years before their 1980 victory. Where were the 1960 games held?

Answer Sheet

Hockey
2 Rolls

Name_____

Answer Sheet

Hockey
2 Rolls

Name_____

Answer Sheet

Hockey
2 Rolls

Name_____

1.	1.	1.
2.	2.	2.
3.	3.	3.
4.	4.	4.
5.	5.	5.
6.	6.	6.
7.	7.	7.
8.	8.	8.
9.	9.	9.
10.	10.	10.

After you have filled out the sheet, fold your column underneath along the dashed line so the next restroom user won't see your answers. *The first player uses the far right column.*

Notes:

Notes:

Notes:

Hockey

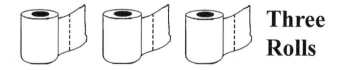

Three Rolls

Flip to pg. 79 for answers

1. In the 1940s, Detroit's Fern Gauthier went down to a Manhattan pier with his hockey stick. What was he trying to prove?

2. What legendary broadcaster went on the air with the words, "Hello Canada and hockey fans in the United States and Newfoundland"? He also coined the phrase, "He shoots, he scores!"

3. What league preceded the formation of the National Hockey League in 1917?

4. Why do hockey players and fans still pay homage to the 16th Earl of Derby?

5. On Feb. 7, 1976, Darryl Sittler of Toronto set an incredible scoring record. What did he do?

6. Why are the New York Rangers called the Rangers?

7. Glenn Hall holds a record for goalies that will never, ever be broken. What is it?

8. Which team that shared Madison Square Garden with the Rangers in the 1920s-1940s officially called themselves "Brooklyn" in 1941-42?

9. Twice in the late 1990s the Stanley Cup was won with a triple-overtime goal. Name one of the goal scorers.

10. Six new teams entered the NHL in 1967-68. Name four of them.

Answer Sheet	Answer Sheet	Answer Sheet
Hockey **3 Rolls**	**Hockey** **3 Rolls**	**Hockey** **3 Rolls**
Name_____	Name_____	Name_____
1.	1.	1.
2.	2.	2.
3.	3.	3.
4.	4.	4.
5.	5.	5.
6.	6.	6.
7.	7.	7.
8.	8.	8.
9.	9.	9.
10.	10.	10.

After you have filled out the sheet, fold your column underneath along the dashed line so the next restroom user won't see your answers. *The first player uses the far right column.*

Notes: *Notes:*   *Notes:*

Golf & Tennis

One Roll

Flip to pg. 80 for answers

1. What color shirt does Tiger Woods wear on Sunday matches?

2. Who has won the most Grand Slam Tennis Championships in men's tennis history?

3. What are the four events that constitute golf's Grand Slam?

4. What surface is the French Open played on?

5. Which golfer has the most Grand Slam wins of all time?

6. What top-ranked rival of Jimmy Connors and Björn Borg is also remembered for asking judges if they were "serious" about their calls?

7. In what city is golf's Masters Tournament held?

8. Who won "The Battle of the Sexes"?

9. What word is yelled to warn other golfers of an errant shot?

10. Who is the US Open stadium in Flushing, New York named for?

Answer Sheet

Golf & Tennis
1 Roll

Name_____

1.	
2.	
3.	
4.	
5.	
6.	
7.	
8.	
9.	
10.	

Answer Sheet

Golf & Tennis
1 Roll

Name_____

1.
2.
3.
4.
5.
6.
7.
8.
9.
10.

Answer Sheet

Golf & Tennis
1 Roll

Name_____

1.
2.
3.
4.
5.
6.
7.
8.
9.
10.

After you have filled out the sheet, fold your column underneath along the dashed line so the next restroom user won't see your answers. *The first player uses the far right column.*

Notes: *Notes:*   *Notes:*

Golf & Tennis

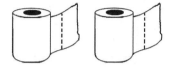

Two Rolls

Flip to pg. 81 for answers

1. Who has won the most Grand Slam Tennis Championships in women's tennis history?

2. Where is the famed "Old Course" located?

3. For what World War I aviator is both the French Open, and the stadium it is played in officially named for?

4. This South African golf superstar usually wore all-black outfits.

5. In the 1920s and 1930s, this American men's champion won 10 Grand Slam Tennis Championships.

6. With 90 international victories, she is simply the winningest ladies golfer ever.

7. John McEnroe's brother was also a tennis player and serves as a TV commentator. What is his first name?

8. Not far from San Francisco, you can play this famous golf course where you hit over the ocean…but it will cost you about $500 to do so.

9. What trophy is played for in nation vs. nation team tennis competition?

10. What type of grass do you usually find on fairways in warmer and tropical climates?

Answer Sheet

Golf & Tennis
2 Rolls

Name_____

1.	
2.	
3.	
4.	
5.	
6.	
7.	
8.	
9.	
10.	

Answer Sheet

Golf & Tennis
2 Rolls

Name_____

1.
2.
3.
4.
5.
6.
7.
8.
9.
10.

Answer Sheet

Golf & Tennis
2 Rolls

Name_____

1.
2.
3.
4.
5.
6.
7.
8.
9.
10.

After you have filled out the sheet, fold your column underneath along the dashed line so the next restroom user won't see your answers. *The first player uses the far right column.*

Notes:

Notes:

Notes:

Golf & Tennis

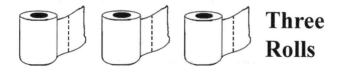

Three Rolls

Flip to pg. 82 for answers

1. If a birdie is one under par, and an eagle is two under par, then what type of bird is a shot that's three under par?

2. Name the Australian Aboriginal who won 7 Grand Slam women's titles.

3. What is a "mashie"?

4. How high is the tennis net at mid-court?

5. A golf superstar of the 1930s-1950s won both the Masters and PGA Championship three times, and the British Open once. But he never won the US Open. Name him.

6. This 1950s-1960s American of Latin descent was the top-ranked men's tennis player in the world for eight straight years.

7. This American woman was not only a champion golfer, but she also won three medals for track & field at the 1932 Summer Olympics.

8. Name the Belgian net star who won the US Open in 2009, a year after giving birth.

9. You and your opponent are both on the green. She does not mark her ball. Your putt hits her ball. Who is penalized?

10. Which President was the first to install a putting green at the White House?

Answer Sheet

Golf & Tennis
3 Rolls

Name_____

Answer Sheet

Golf & Tennis
3 Rolls

Name_____

Answer Sheet

Golf & Tennis
3 Rolls

Name_____

1.	1.	1.
2.	2.	2.
3.	3.	3.
4.	4.	4.
5.	5.	5.
6.	6.	6.
7.	7.	7.
8.	8.	8.
9.	9.	9.
10.	10.	10.

After you have filled out the sheet, fold your column underneath along the dashed line so the next restroom user won't see your answers. *The first player uses the far right column.*

Notes: *Notes:*   *Notes:*

Rules

 One Roll

Flip to pg. 83 for answers

1. What colored card gets you kicked out of a soccer game?

2. In baseball, what does the umpire call if the pitcher does something to deceive a runner on base?

3. In darts, how many throws does a player get per round?

4. How many steps can a basketball player take before being whistled for traveling?

5. If a tennis player's serve hits the top of the net, and then lands in the proper box, what is the ruling?

6. How many football players are allowed on the field at one time?

7. In boxing, what does T.K.O. stand for?

8. What is the heaviest ball a bowler can use in competition?

9. What is the call in hockey when a player tangles the stick in an opponent's skates, causing that player to fall to the ice?

10. Sometimes 100-meter dash sprinters try to jump the gun. When this happens, two gunshots are usually heard. What does that indicate?

Answer Sheet | Answer Sheet | Answer Sheet

Answer Sheet | Answer Sheet

Rules
1 Roll

Rules
1 Roll

Rules
1 Roll

Name_____ Name_____ Name_____

1.	1.	1.
2.	2.	2.
3.	3.	3.
4.	4.	4.
5.	5.	5.
6.	6.	6.
7.	7.	7.
8.	8.	8.
9.	9.	9.
10.	10.	10.

After you have filled out the sheet, fold your column underneath along the dashed line so the next restroom user won't see your answers. *The first player uses the far right column.*

Notes: | *Notes:* | *Notes:*

Rules

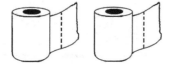 **Two Rolls**

Flip to pg. 84 for answers

1. How many points are needed to win a set-tie-breaker in tennis?

2. In hockey, a defenseman falls on the puck in the goal crease. What is the ruling?

3. In pool, what is the common name for a foul committed when a player pockets the cue ball?

4. What is ruled when a defending soccer player kicks the ball behind his team's own goal line?

5. Unlike the NBA, NCAA basketball players are ejected after this many fouls.

6. What does a football referee call when a distressed quarterback throws the ball nowhere near a receiver?

7. What is called in hockey when a goalie shoots the puck over the side glass?

8. What is the penalty for a golfer who hits the ball out of bounds?

9. How many players can be on a baseball playoff roster?

10. In basketball, how far away from the basket is the free-throw line?

Answer Sheet

Rules
2 Rolls

Name_____

Answer Sheet

Rules
2 Rolls

Name_____

Answer Sheet

Rules
2 Rolls

Name_____

1.	1.	1.
2.	2.	2.
3.	3.	3.
4.	4.	4.
5.	5.	5.
6.	6.	6.
7.	7.	7.
8.	8.	8.
9.	9.	9.
10.	10.	10.

After you have filled out the sheet, fold your column underneath along the dashed line so the next restroom user won't see your answers. *The first player uses the far right column.*

Notes: *Notes:*   *Notes:*

41

Rules

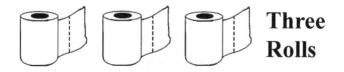

Three Rolls

Flip to pg. 85 for answers

1. How many clubs can a golfer legally carry in a bag?

2. With the bases loaded and one out, a batter pops the ball up to the shortstop. What does the umpire immediately call?

3. What rule did the NHL get rid of in 2005 when they diminished the role of the center-ice red line?

4. Within one year, what is the maximum age for a Scripps National Spelling Bee competitor?

5. What is the lightest weight class in Mixed Martial Arts?

6. How many officials are there in an NFL game?

7. Besides running with it, what is the only way to legally move the ball forward in Rugby League or Rugby Union?

8. What are the dimensions of a hockey net? If you reverse it, it is the same size as a baseball batter's box.

9. The NBA and WNBA both use a 24-second shot-clock. NCAA Men's Basketball uses a 35-second clock. What is the shot-clock in NCAA Women's Basketball?

10. What stick-sport does not permit the use of left-handed sticks in competition?

Answer Sheet

Rules
3 Rolls

Name_____

Answer Sheet

Rules
3 Rolls

Name_____

Answer Sheet

Rules
3 Rolls

Name_____

1.	1.	1.
2.	2.	2.
3.	3.	3.
4.	4.	4.
5.	5.	5.
6.	6.	6.
7.	7.	7.
8.	8.	8.
9.	9.	9.
10.	10.	10.

After you have filled out the sheet, fold your column underneath along the dashed line so the next restroom user won't see your answers. *The first player uses the far right column.*

Notes: *Notes:*   *Notes:*

Racing—All Kinds

Flip to pg. 86 for answers

 One Roll

1. What winter sport is Apolo Ohno famous for?

2. The "World's Fastest Man" is this Jamaican sprinter who set world records in both the 100 and 200-meter dashes.

3. Traditionally, what beverage is enjoyed by drivers who win the Indianapolis 500?

4. What are the three legs of the Triple Crown of Thoroughbred Racing?

5. What numbered car did Dale Earnhardt drive most of his career?

6. What English runner was the first to break the 4-minute mile in 1954?

7. This record-setting Olympic swimming champion was also famous for his diet that consisted of 12,000 calories a day. That's 1,500 calories for every gold medal he won in 2008.

8. With 200 career NASCAR victories, he is the winningest driver in history.

9. What color jersey does the leader of the Tour de France wear?

10. How many miles constitute a marathon?

Answer Sheet

Racing—All Kinds
1 Roll

Name_____

1.	
2.	
3.	
4.	
5.	
6.	
7.	
8.	
9.	
10.	

Answer Sheet

Racing—All Kinds
1 Roll

Name_____

1.	
2.	
3.	
4.	
5.	
6.	
7.	
8.	
9.	
10.	

Answer Sheet

Racing—All Kinds
1 Roll

Name_____

1.	
2.	
3.	
4.	
5.	
6.	
7.	
8.	
9.	
10.	

After you have filled out the sheet, fold your column underneath along the dashed line so the next restroom user won't see your answers. *The first player uses the far right column.*

Notes: *Notes:*   *Notes:*

Racing—All Kinds

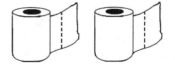

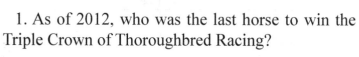 **Two Rolls**

Flip to pg. 87 for answers

1. As of 2012, who was the last horse to win the Triple Crown of Thoroughbred Racing?

2. What famous run takes place on Patriots' Day every April?

3. What yacht race claims to have the oldest active trophy in international sports?

4. He won an incredible five straight NASCAR Sprint Cup Series Championships between 2006-2010.

5. Name the American swimmer who won seven gold medals—the record at the time—at the 1972 Munich Olympic Games.

6. How far is the final track race in a decathlon?

7. Three drivers have won the Indianapolis 500 four times. Name one of them.

8. What were the first stock cars trying to outrace?

9. What is the starting point of the New York City Marathon?

10. She won three gold medals in sprinting for the US in the 1960 Summer Olympics in Rome.

Answer Sheet

Racing—All Kinds
2 Rolls

Name_____

1.
2.
3.
4.
5.
6.
7.
8.
9.
10.

Answer Sheet

Racing—All Kinds
2 Rolls

Name_____

1.
2.
3.
4.
5.
6.
7.
8.
9.
10.

Answer Sheet

Racing—All Kinds
2 Rolls

Name_____

1.
2.
3.
4.
5.
6.
7.
8.
9.
10.

After you have filled out the sheet, fold your column underneath along the dashed line so the next restroom user won't see your answers. *The first player uses the far right column.*

Notes:

Notes:

Notes:

Racing—All Kinds

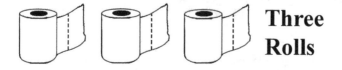

Three Rolls

Flip to pg. 88 for answers

1. What college team did Steve Prefontaine run for?

2. Since 1975, what famous street has the Tour de France finished on?

3. This Norwegian won nine New York City Marathons, the most ever by any woman in the race.

4. A 2.4-mile swim, 112-mile bike, and a marathon run are the three legs that make up what grueling competition?

5. One of the legs of the Triple Crown of Harness Racing for Trotters, this race is held at Meadowlands Racetrack every August.

6. From 1963-1977, this NASCAR driver finished 1-2 with Richard Petty 63 times.

7. Very popular in the US before World War II, this type of race tied up venues such as Madison Square Garden for several days.

8. What are foot races in duration of 50, 100, or even 1,000 miles long classified as?

9. This Italian-American driver has won in just about every racing form you can think of, including Indy Cars, Formula One, sprint, sports, and dirt track cars. He took the checkered flag at the 1969 Indianapolis 500. Can you name him?

10. Moroccan runner Hicham El Guerrouj has held the world record in the mile since 1999. Within five seconds, how fast did he run?

Answer Sheet | Answer Sheet | Answer Sheet

Racing—All Kinds
3 Rolls

Racing—All Kinds
3 Rolls

Racing—All Kinds
3 Rolls

Name_____ Name_____ Name_____

1.	1.	1.
2.	2.	2.
3.	3.	3.
4.	4.	4.
5.	5.	5.
6.	6.	6.
7.	7.	7.
8.	8.	8.
9.	9.	9.
10.	10.	10.

After you have filled out the sheet, fold your column underneath along the dashed line so the next restroom user won't see your answers. *The first player uses the far right column.*

Notes: | *Notes:* | *Notes:*

Personalities

One Roll

Flip to pg. 89 for answers

1. What Basketball Hall of Fame rebounding machine kept fans guessing what color his hair would be on a given night?

2. Who is the all-time leader in baseball stolen bases? Rather than cash a million dollar bonus check, he hung it on his wall to remind himself that he was a millionaire.

3. The most feared enforcer of the Philadelphia Flyers "Broad Street Bullies" team of the 1970s, he still holds the record for most penalty minutes in a season with 472 in 1974-75.

4. Introduced in wrestling matches to be 7 feet 4 inches tall, this former champion also starred in the movie *The Princess Bride*.

5. Who won the Tour de France an incredible seven times in a row from 1999-2005?

6. This hot-tempered college basketball coach is known more for throwing chairs than for winning championships with the Indiana Hoosiers.

7. He had multiple world records in his day as a sprinter and jumper. But if you were at that Nets home game in 1993 to hear him sing the National Anthem, you would have run for the hills!

8. What golfer from Puerto Rico would make a birdie putt, and then dance with his putter as if it was a sword?

9. This seven-time Cy Young Award winner threw a broken bat near Mike Piazza in Game 2 of the 2000 World Series.

10. Mike Tyson once took a bite out of which boxer's right ear?

Answer Sheet

Personalities
1 Roll

Name_____

Answer Sheet

Personalities
1 Roll

Name_____

Answer Sheet

Personalities
1 Roll

Name_____

1.	1.	1.
2.	2.	2.
3.	3.	3.
4.	4.	4.
5.	5.	5.
6.	6.	6.
7.	7.	7.
8.	8.	8.
9.	9.	9.
10.	10.	10.

After you have filled out the sheet, fold your column underneath along the dashed line so the next restroom user won't see your answers. *The first player uses the far right column.*

Notes: *Notes:*   *Notes:*

Personalities

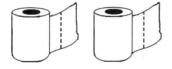

Two Rolls

Flip to pg. 90 for answers

1. Who was the captain of the 1980 "Miracle on Ice" team? He scored the winning goal in the epic game against the Soviet Union.

2. Brazilian soccer player Edison "Edson" Arantes do Nascimento is better known as what bicycle-kicking champion?

3. After ten failed attempts, this skateboarder landed a "900" (a 900 degree 2.5-revolution aerial spin) at the 1999 X-Games.

4. Exasperated by his New York Mets finding new ways to lose, he exclaimed, "Can't anybody here play this game?"

5. Name this mean-spirited baseball Hall of Famer who was known to sharpen his spikes before games.

6. This tennis great once planned to marry Jimmy Connors, and later did marry Greg Norman.

7. Real-life hockey players Jeff Carlson and Steve Carlson were two of these three whacko brothers in the movie *Slap Shot*.

8. This "king" of golf is also one of its greatest ambassadors. He designed the first new golf course in China after it became Communist.

9. Millions of people saw her in a sports-bra after she scored the winning shootout kick at the 1999 FIFA Women's World Cup.

10. This man's home runs were said to be fueled by hot dogs and beer, not steroids.

Answer Sheet

Personalities
2 Rolls

Name_____

1.

2.

3.

4.

5.

6.

7.

8.

9.

10.

Answer Sheet

Personalities
2 Rolls

Name_____

1.

2.

3.

4.

5.

6.

7.

8.

9.

10.

Answer Sheet

Personalities
2 Rolls

Name_____

1.

2.

3.

4.

5.

6.

7.

8.

9.

10.

After you have filled out the sheet, fold your column underneath along the dashed line so the next restroom user won't see your answers. *The first player uses the far right column.*

Notes:

Notes:

Notes:

Personalities

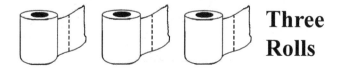

Three Rolls

Flip to pg. 91 for answers

1. Regarded as one of the greatest Argentine soccer players of all time, this legend came back to coach Argentina in the 2010 FIFA World Cup.

2. Born Richard Raskind, this tennis player had a sex change operation and played on the women's circuit in the 1970s.

3. Name the pro golfer who was said to hustle bets by using a Dr. Pepper bottle as a putter.

4. Known as "Night Train," this star NFL defensive back of the 1950s and 1960s was married to jazz singer Dinah Washington.

5. It was said that this "cool" Negro League baseball star was so fast he would turn off the light switch and get into bed before the room got dark.

6. Your goose is cooked! The first "clown prince" of basketball starred for both the Harlem Globetrotters and Fabulous Harlem Magicians.

7. Nicknamed the "Bucharest Buffoon," this Romanian tennis great was known for "nasty" antics on the court.

8. Name the Stanley Cup-winning goaltender of the 1980s who considered the crease to be his personal domain. He was known to whack opponents who visited it.

9. This great, hairless Green Bay Packers linebacker took several hard passes in the groin from Burt Reynolds in the original production of *The Longest Yard*.

10. This funny player and announcer is probably the only person in Major League Baseball history to pull his pants down after legging out an infield single.

# Answer Sheet	# Answer Sheet	# Answer Sheet
Personalities **3 Rolls**	**Personalities** **3 Rolls**	**Personalities** **3 Rolls**
Name_____	Name_____	Name_____
1.	1.	1.
2.	2.	2.
3.	3.	3.
4.	4.	4.
5.	5.	5.
6.	6.	6.
7.	7.	7.
8.	8.	8.
9.	9.	9.
10.	10.	10.

After you have filled out the sheet, fold your column underneath along the dashed line so the next restroom user won't see your answers. *The first player uses the far right column.*

Notes:

Notes:

Notes:

Famous Firsts

 One Roll

Flip to pg. 92 for answers

1. What was Montreal hockey goalie Jacques Plante the first to wear in 1959? He did not wear it on Friday the 13th.

2. Who was the first pitcher to strikeout 20 batters in a Major League Baseball game?

3. "Sir Barton" wasn't human, but he was the first to win this in 1919 with three victories as thousands cheered.

4. Who hit the first home run at old Yankee Stadium?

5. The first Winter Olympics held in the US were staged here in 1932. There was a return engagement in 1980.

6. May Sutton Bundy was the first American individual to travel across the pond, racket in hand, to win this in 1905.

7. This trophy was awarded for the first time in 1893 when it was won by the Montreal Amateur Athletic Association.

8. What Major League Baseball team was the first to play its home games indoors?

9. Who was the first head coach of the Dallas Cowboys?

10. In 1969, this running back with the first name of Orenthal was the first player chosen in the common AFL/NFL draft.

Answer Sheet

Famous Firsts
1 Roll

Name_____

Answer Sheet

Famous Firsts
1 Roll

Name_____

Answer Sheet

Famous Firsts
1 Roll

Name_____

1.	1.	1.
2.	2.	2.
3.	3.	3.
4.	4.	4.
5.	5.	5.
6.	6.	6.
7.	7.	7.
8.	8.	8.
9.	9.	9.
10.	10.	10.

After you have filled out the sheet, fold your column underneath along the dashed line so the next restroom user won't see your answers. ***The first player uses the far right column.***

Notes: *Notes:* *Notes:*

Famous Firsts

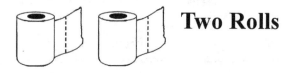

Two Rolls

Flip to pg. 93 for answers

1. Within five points for each team, what was the score of the first Super Bowl in 1967?

2. After Joe DiMaggio hit safely in 56 consecutive games, who was the first player to reach 40 consecutive games?

3. Who was the head coach that led Notre Dame to their first national title with a victory in the 1925 Rose Bowl?

4. Who won the first World Series?

5. Who was the first player chosen in the 1984 NBA draft, which saw Michael Jordan go to Chicago with the third pick? He was a Hall of Fame center for the Houston Rockets.

6. Who was the first African American to play in the American League?

7. This Norwegian was the first woman to win the Olympic gold medal in figure skating three times. She later toured the US in traveling ice shows and appeared in Hollywood films.

8. Johnny Moss "cleaned up" in 1970 and 1971 to become the first winner of what strategic tournament?

9. Who was the first defenseman to lead the NHL in scoring?

10. What was the first post-1961 expansion team to win a World Series?

Answer Sheet

Famous Firsts
2 Rolls

Name_____

1.
2.
3.
4.
5.
6.
7.
8.
9.
10.

Answer Sheet

Famous Firsts
2 Rolls

Name_____

1.
2.
3.
4.
5.
6.
7.
8.
9.
10.

Answer Sheet

Famous Firsts
2 Rolls

Name_____

1.
2.
3.
4.
5.
6.
7.
8.
9.
10.

After you have filled out the sheet, fold your column underneath along the dashed line so the next restroom user won't see your answers. ***The first player uses the far right column.***

Notes:

Notes:

Notes:

Famous Firsts

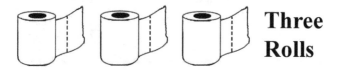

Three Rolls

Flip to pg. 94 for answers

1. Who was the first NFL kicker to knock a 60+ yard field goal through the uprights?

2. Who was the first woman to swim the English Channel?

3. Who was the first American to score 50 goals in an NHL season?

4. Who made the first oversized tennis racket?

5. What was the first basketball team to be known as Celtics?

6. Who was the first African American in the National Hockey League?

7. Which President was the first to throw out the ceremonial first pitch on Opening Day of the baseball season?

8. What was Wayne Gretzky's first professional hockey team? It wasn't the Edmonton Oilers.

9. Who was the first heavyweight champion to lose, and then regain his title?

10. What team hosted the first night game in Major League Baseball history on May 24, 1935?

Answer Sheet

Famous Firsts
3 Rolls

Name_____

Answer Sheet

Famous Firsts
3 Rolls

Name_____

Answer Sheet

Famous Firsts
3 Rolls

Name_____

1.	1.	1.
2.	2.	2.
3.	3.	3.
4.	4.	4.
5.	5.	5.
6.	6.	6.
7.	7.	7.
8.	8.	8.
9.	9.	9.
10.	10.	10.

After you have filled out the sheet, fold your column underneath along the dashed line so the next restroom user won't see your answers. *The first player uses the far right column.*

Notes:

Notes:

Notes:

Everything & Anything

 One Roll

Flip to pg. 95 for answers

1. What sport uses a shuttlecock, or birdie?

2. If you bet the first two horses in order, it's called an exacta. If you bet the first three in order, it's called a trifecta. What is it called when you bet the first four to finish in order?

3. Boasting 19 league titles, this organization calls itself the most popular soccer team in the world.

4. How many points are needed to win an individual game of table tennis?

5. In what sport do horses leap fences?

6. What sport features a competitor attempting a Triple Axel?

7. This aquatic team sport does not involve horses.

8. What boxer became more famous for his grill?

9. What position on a volleyball court is responsible for giving soft touches for attackers to spike?

10. Traditionally, what color is a box of Wheaties?

Answer Sheet

Everything & Anything
1 Roll

Name_____

Answer Sheet

Everything & Anything
1 Roll

Name_____

Answer Sheet

Everything & Anything
1 Roll

Name_____

1.	1.	1.
2.	2.	2.
3.	3.	3.
4.	4.	4.
5.	5.	5.
6.	6.	6.
7.	7.	7.
8.	8.	8.
9.	9.	9.
10.	10.	10.

After you have filled out the sheet, fold your column underneath along the dashed line so the next restroom user won't see your answers. *The first player uses the far right column.*

Notes: *Notes:*   *Notes:*

Everything & Anything

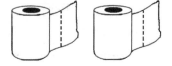

Two Rolls

Flip to pg. 96 for answers

1. What winter event similar to bobsledding involves competitors racing feet first on a one or two-person sled?

2. Name three of the four events in traditional all-around women's gymnastics.

3. What type of skiing involves bumps along the downhill?

4. How many players take the field for a cricket team?

5. If you were in Dublin, you might watch this game played by 15 on a side, where the object is to kick or hit a ball with your hand into the goal.

6. Nicknamed, "The World's Most Dangerous Man," this former professional wrestler is now a member of the UFC Hall of Fame. Who is he?

7. What name is given to the bullfighter who kills the bull?

8. If you watched this water sport, you might see the competitors' legs flapping in unison above the pool line.

9. This two-part weightlifting event involves first getting the bar to the clavicles or shoulders, and then lifting it over the head. One might say this event sounds like an insult.

10. What game, once popular in ancient Rome, is divided into scoring periods known as giri. It's played with one small ball, and eight larger ones.

Answer Sheet

Everything & Anything
2 Rolls

Name_____

1.
2.
3.
4.
5.
6.
7.
8.
9.
10.

Answer Sheet

Everything & Anything
2 Rolls

Name_____

1.
2.
3.
4.
5.
6.
7.
8.
9.
10.

Answer Sheet

Everything & Anything
2 Rolls

Name_____

1.
2.
3.
4.
5.
6.
7.
8.
9.
10.

After you have filled out the sheet, fold your column underneath along the dashed line so the next restroom user won't see your answers. *The first player uses the far right column.*

Notes: *Notes:*   *Notes:*

Everything & Anything

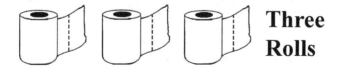

Three Rolls

Flip to pg. 97 for answers

1. What winter favorite is more than just "shuffle-board on ice"?

2. In rowing, what is the name of the person who yells at the rowers?

3. What split in bowling leaves the two corner pins to be dealt with?

4. What winter sport has the unique combination of both cross-country skiing and rifle-shooting?

5. As of 2012, what stadium in the US has the largest seating capacity?

6. What sport involves gymnastics, dance, and acrobatics on horses?

7. One of the best basketball teams in the 1920s was known as the "SPHAs." What did the letters stand for?

8. Within ¼ inch, how thick is the ice on a hockey rink?

9. What German was knocked out by Joe Louis in the Heavyweight Championship fight on June 22, 1938 at Yankee Stadium?

10. In baseball, what is the maximum number of hits a team can get in an inning without scoring a run?

Answer Sheet | Answer Sheet | Answer Sheet

Everything & Anything
3 Rolls

Everything & Anything
3 Rolls

Everything & Anything
3 Rolls

Name_____ Name_____ Name_____

1.	1.	1.
2.	2.	2.
3.	3.	3.
4.	4.	4.
5.	5.	5.
6.	6.	6.
7.	7.	7.
8.	8.	8.
9.	9.	9.
10.	10.	10.

After you have filled out the sheet, fold your column underneath along the dashed line so the next restroom user won't see your answers. *The first player uses the far right column.*

Notes:　　　　*Notes:*　　　　*Notes:*

Football

 ## One Roll — Answers

1. Brett Favre - 71,838 yards

2. Scott Norwood. The Giants won the game 20-19.

3. Steve Young

4. William "The Refrigerator" Perry

5. Deion Sanders played part-time for the Yankees, Braves, Reds, and Giants. He had a career batting average of .263 with 39 home runs, and 186 stolen bases.

6. Howard Cosell

7. Red Grange

8. Barry Sanders retired in 1999 with 15,629 yards. He is currently ranked third behind Emmitt Smith and Walter Payton.

9. Ben Roethlisberger, Super Bowl XL

10. Canton, Ohio

Football

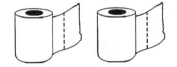

Two Rolls — Answers

1. New Orleans Saints, Houston Oilers, Minnesota Vikings

2. Roger Staubach

3. The Baltimore Colts defeated the New York Giants 23-17 in the NFL Championship Game. The game went to sudden-death overtime, and was won on a short run by Alan "The Horse" Ameche.

4. *Heidi*. With the Jets leading by three points, fans in Eastern and Central time zones lost the feed to the game. As the Raiders came back to ultimately win 43-32, NBC was flooded with calls from angry football fans. Besides showing how popular football had become, the fiasco changed the way games would be subsequently televised.

5. Leon Lett

6. Fog. The game was known as the "Fog Bowl," after a dense fog rolled into Soldier Field off of Lake Michigan. The players complained that they couldn't even see the sidelines.

7. Boise State

8. Jim Brown

9. New York Jets 16, Baltimore Colts 7. The victory was guaranteed by Joe Namath.

10. Dan Marino - 61,361 yards

Football

Three Rolls — Answers

1. Herm Edwards of the Philadelphia Eagles. All the New York Giants had to do was run out the clock by taking a knee. But instead, quarterback Joe Pisarcik attempted a handoff to Larry Csonka. The botched exchange was recovered by Edwards who ran for the winning score.

2. A missed field goal attempt. Ryan Longwell of the Vikings missed a 58-yard field goal at the Metrodome. Cromartie fielded the ball about two inches in front of the end line, and ran farther than any player before him. Several players had been tied with 108 yards before the runback.

3. Wrigley Field

4. All-America Football Conference (AAFC)

5. Vince Lombardi

6. On Dec. 8, 1940, the Chicago Bears defeated the Washington Redskins 73-0 in the NFL Championship Game. It is the largest margin of victory in any NFL game, regular season or playoff. When Redskins quarterback Sammy Baugh was asked if the outcome would have been different had his receiver not dropped a pass in the end zone, his answer was, "Sure. The final score would have been 73-7."

7. 110 yards. Each end zone is 20 yards, so the length of the entire field is 150 yards.

8. Mike Ditka and Tom Flores

9. They were the Chicago Cardinals before 1960, and the St. Louis Cardinals from 1960-1987

10. 222. Georgia Tech defeated Cumberland University 222-0 on October 7, 1916.

Baseball

One Roll — Answers

1. He got his 4,192nd career hit off of San Diego's Eric Show, passing Ty Cobb on the all-time hit parade

2. Joe DiMaggio in 1941

3. The Houston Colt .45s. They were not called the Astros until 1965.

4. Nolan Ryan with 5,714

5. Fenway Park. Johnny Pesky wasn't known for his power. But, legend has him sneaking a few home runs inside the right field foul pole, located just 302 feet from home plate.

6. Lou Gehrig

7. Chicago Cubs

8. George Brett

9. Boston Red Sox (1918-2004), Chicago White Sox (1917-2005)

10. A ground ball was hit to the second baseman, who threw to the first baseman for the out

Baseball

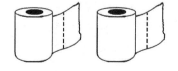 **Two Rolls — Answers**

1. Earl Weaver

2. Larry

3. Shea Stadium

4. Rube

5. Carlos Beltrán. He also tied Barry Bonds' 2002 record of 8 home runs in a single postseason.

6. Phil Niekro

7. Ted Williams

8. Josh Gibson

9. Frank Robinson. He won with the Cincinnati Reds in 1961 and the Baltimore Orioles in 1966. As far as the epic home run is concerned, a flag saying "Here" marked the supposed spot of the mammoth blast.

10. Mariano Rivera

Baseball

Three Rolls — Answers

1. Polo Grounds

2. Hideo Nomo. He did it twice. First for the Dodgers against the Colorado Rockies on September 17, 1996, and then for the Boston Red Sox against the Baltimore Orioles on April 4, 2001.

3. Mark Buehrle

4. Duke Snider with 326. His Brooklyn Dodger teammate, Gil Hodges, is second with 310.

5. War Memorial Stadium

6. Don Denkinger

7. Hank Aaron, Stan Musial, and Willie Mays. It should be noted that between 1959-62, there were two All-Star games each season.

8. Al "Sparky" Lyle

9. John Franco

10. Chuck Connors

Basketball

 ## One Roll — Answers

1. Wilt Chamberlain. He scored 100 points for the Philadelphia Warriors against the New York Knicks on March 2, 1962 at the Hersheypark Arena in Hershey, Pennsylvania. In those days, many NBA teams "farmed out" home games to other nearby venues.

2. Red Auerbach

3. The "Dream Team." With a team made up of Michael Jordan, Larry Bird, Charles Barkley, Magic Johnson, and a host of other future Hall of Famers, who's to doubt the name? In their first contest, they defeated Angola 116-48. From there, they cruised to a gold medal.

4. UCLA—11

5. Chris Webber. After almost traveling, Webber made the error and North Carolina won the game.

6. Boston Celtics—17 Championships, and 21 retired numbers. If the trend continues, they will be hanging triple-digit jerseys from the rafters. Even 00 is retired (Robert Parish).

7. Julius Erving

8. University of Connecticut Huskies Women's Basketball Team. They broke the old mark of 88 set by John Wooden's UCLA Men's Teams from 1971-74. The Huskies run lasted from 2008 until 2010. They lost to Stanford a week later after reaching 90 wins.

9. Lew Alcindor

10. 23 and 45

Basketball

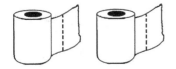 **Two Rolls — Answers**

1. "Pistol Pete" Maravich for LSU. He scored 3,667 points in just three varsity seasons. Back then, freshmen weren't allowed to play on varsity.

2. John Starks

3. John Havlicek. Johnny Most, the gravel-voiced announcer for the Boston Celtics, screamed over and over that "Havlicek stole the ball!"

4. Tim Duncan (2002, 2003), Steve Nash (2005-2006), LeBron James (2009-2010)

5. Indiana State

6. Washington Generals. Though the Generals beat the Globetrotters a few times, they have lost more than 13,000 contests. By the way, did you know that the Globetrotters didn't start in Harlem? They were founded by Abe Saperstein in Chicago in 1926.

7. George Mikan

8. Bill Laimbeer

9. Orlando Magic, Los Angeles Lakers, Miami Heat, Phoenix Suns, Cleveland Cavaliers, Boston Celtics

10. New York Knicks

Basketball

Three Rolls — Answers

1. Oscar Robertson. "The Big O" averaged 30.8 points, 12.5 rebounds, and 11.4 assists for the Cincinnati Royals in the 1961-62 season.

2. Manute Bol, 7 feet 7 inches, and Muggsy Bogues, 5 feet 3 inches. Bol is tied with Gheorghe Mureşan who was also listed at 7 feet 7 inches.

3. Texas Western

4. Cynthia Cooper of the Houston Comets. The Comets won the first four titles from 1997-2000.

5. They were the widely-imitated public address announcers for the Knicks and Warriors (later 76ers) respectively

6. Syracuse Nationals

7. City College of New York (CCNY)

8. Holy Cross

9. Philadelphia Warriors

10. Maurice Podoloff, who was the league's president from its inception in 1946 until 1963

Hockey

One Roll — Answers

1. Montreal Canadiens—24

2. Boston Bruins, Chicago Blackhawks, Detroit Red Wings, Montreal Canadiens, New York Rangers, Toronto Maple Leafs. They are not really the first six teams, just the only ones from 1942-43 through 1966-67.

3. 99

4. An octopus. The tradition started on April 15, 1952 when brothers, and fish merchants, Pete and Jerry Cusimano, threw one on the ice. The eight tentacles symbolized the eight wins needed to win a Stanley Cup in those days.

5. Toronto. That's where the "real" Stanley Cup is. The original bowl is on display with quite a few rogue engravings and scratches on it. The one that you see every June is not the one that Lord Stanley bought for about $50. Down through the years, either Cup has been lost, stolen, drop-kicked into a canal, gone swimming, and (reportedly) used as a baby toilet and urinal. Still, players love to kiss it.

6. Neutral zone

7. Five

8. FOX. They used "FoxTrax" to highlight a puck. On really powerful slapshots, it would have a red tail like a comet.

9. Bobby and Brett Hull

10. Martin Brodeur of the New Jersey Devils. He also holds the NHL records for most minutes played in a season, wins in a season, overtime wins, overall minutes, and most consecutive 30-win seasons.

Hockey

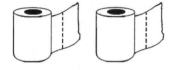 **Two Rolls — Answers**

1. The Montreal Forum. The old Montreal Maroons played there first, beginning in 1924.

2. There was a worldwide flu epidemic. Montreal's Bad Joe Hall died of it, and the final series was stopped.

3. Vladislav Tretiak. In a radical move to shake up his team against the US in the 1980 Olympics, Soviet coach Viktor Tikhonov pulled Tretiak after letting up a goal in the last second of the 1st period. Had he stayed in, there may not have been a "Miracle on Ice."

4. Danny Gallivan

5. Boston Bruins. They started play in 1924-25.

6. Gordie Howe with 801. Gretzky finished with 894.

7. Mike Bossy

8. Goaltender. The trophy is named for Montreal goaltender Georges Vézina, who died of tuberculosis on March 27, 1926, a few months after collapsing in the goal crease.

9. Three. The fastest hat trick ever recorded.

10. Squaw Valley, California

.

Hockey

Three Rolls — Answers

1. That he could shoot the puck in the ocean. Gauthier was actually being a good sport in helping out a *Detroit Times* writer. He allowed the scribe to report that he missed his first two shots, the first being snatched by an airborne seagull, and the second landing on a moving barge.

2. Toronto Maple Leafs broadcaster Foster Hewitt. He called his first game way back in 1923.

3. National Hockey Association (NHA)

4. More people remember him as Lord Stanley of Preston, the donator of the Stanley Cup. By the way, his first name was Frederick.

5. He notched 10 points in one game: 6 goals and 4 assists. Toronto beat Boston 11-4.

6. Madison Square Garden president George "Tex" Rickard admired the Texas Rangers (the lawmen, not the baseball team) as a kid. So the team became known as "Tex's Rangers."

7. Most consecutive games played. The former Detroit and Chicago goaltender played in 502 consecutive games. That's over seven seasons without a day off between the pipes. He was known to vomit before every game.

8. New York Americans

9. Uwe Krupp for the Colorado Avalanche in 1996, and Brett Hull for the Dallas Stars in 1999. Sabres fans still feel the latter was "no-goal."

10. California Seals, Los Angeles Kings, Minnesota North Stars, Philadelphia Flyers, Pittsburgh Penguins, St. Louis Blues

Golf & Tennis

 One Roll — Answers

1. Red

2. Roger Federer—17. 5 US Open titles, 7 Wimbledon titles, 1 French Open title, 4 Australian Open titles.

3. Masters Golf Tournament, US Open, British Open, PGA Championship

4. Clay

5. Jack Nicklaus—18

6. John McEnroe

7. Augusta, Georgia

8. Billy Jean King defeated Bobby Riggs at the Astrodome on September 20, 1973. Riggs, a former tennis champion, was 55 when he lost to King, 6-4, 6-3, 6-3. King took home a $100,000 prize.

9. Fore! There are different etymologies for the word. It's most likely derived from either a warning to artillery troops to keep their heads down during battle, or caution to "forecaddies" that would stand a distance in front of the golfer in the early years of the sport.

10. Arthur Ashe

Golf & Tennis

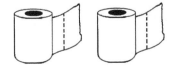

Two Rolls — Answers

1. Margaret Smith Court—24. 5 US Open Titles, 3 Wimbledon Titles, 5 French Open Titles, 11 Australian Open Titles.

2. St. Andrews, Scotland

3. Roland Garros

4. Gary Player

5. Bill Tilden

6. Annika Sörenstam

7. Patrick

8. Pebble Beach Golf Links

9. Davis Cup

10. Bermuda grass

Golf & Tennis

Three Rolls — Answers

1. Albatross. But more people simply call it a "double eagle."

2. Evonne Goolagong

3. The old name for a mid-range iron. If you said anything from 4-6 iron, you are correct.

4. 36 inches

5. Sam Snead

6. Pancho Gonzales

7. Mildred "Babe" Didrikson Zaharias. She was also a basketball All-American, and an expert baseball and softball player, diver, and bowler. She said she earned the nickname "Babe" after hitting five home runs in a children's baseball game, although her mother had called her that for years.

8. Kim Clijsters

9. Your opponent is penalized two shots in Medal (Stroke) Play. In Match Play, you win the hole.

10. Dwight D. Eisenhower

Rules

 ## One Roll — Answers

1. Red

2. Balk

3. Three

4. Two

5. It's a "let," and since it landed in the proper box, it's still the first
.ervice

6. Eleven. Twelve if you are playing Canadian Football.

7. Technical Knockout

8. Sixteen pounds

9. Tripping

10. False-start

Rules

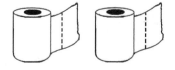 **Two Rolls — Answers**

1. Seven. However, the winning player must win by two. In some tournaments there is no seven-point tiebreaker in the final set, and games are played until someone wins by two. This can go on forever. In 2010, John Isner defeated Nicolas Mahut in a five-set Wimbledon match that took three days to complete. Isner won the last set 70-68 in what became the longest match in tennis history.

2. Penalty shot

3. Scratch

4. Corner kick

5. Five. In the NBA, players foul out after six.

6. Intentional grounding. Ten yard penalty and loss of down.

7. Delay of game penalty

8. One stroke penalty plus loss of distance. So if you slice your drive out of bounds, you will hit your next shot from the tee box, but it will be your third stroke.

9. Twenty-five

10. Fifteen feet

Rules

Three Rolls — Answers

1. 14, which includes the putter

2. Infield fly rule. The batter is out, and the runners can advance at their own risk.

3. Offside pass, often called a "two-line pass"

4. Fifteen. A contestant can enter if they have not reached their 15th birthday by August 31.

5. Flyweight, under 125 lbs

6. Seven. Referee, umpire, head linesman, field judge, line judge, back judge, side judge.

7. By kicking it. The forward pass is illegal.

8. 4 feet x 6 feet

9. 30 seconds

10. Field hockey, as if lefties didn't have it hard enough already. Left-handed sticks are sometimes produced by manufacturers, but are rather difficult to find.

Racing—All Kinds

 ## One Roll — Answers

1. Short track speed skating

2. Usain Bolt

3. Milk. They don't always celebrate with it, though. In 1993 Emerson Fittipaldi drank orange juice instead.

4. Kentucky Derby, Preakness Stakes, Belmont Stakes

5. #3 car

6. Roger Bannister

7. Michael Phelps

8. Richard Petty. However, he and Dale Earnhardt are tied with seven Championships each.

9. Yellow

10. 26.2 miles. Greek legend has Pheidippides running about 25 miles from Marathon to Athens to give word of the Greek victory over the Persians. In 490 BC, he yelled, "Nike!" for victory, and then died from exhaustion shortly afterward. And yes, Nike means "victory" in Greek.

Racing—All Kinds

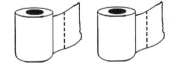

Two Rolls — Answers

1. Affirmed in 1978

2. Boston Marathon

3. America's Cup was first awarded in 1851

4. Jimmie Johnson

5. Mark Spitz

6. 1500 meters

7. A.J. Foyt, Al Unser, Rick Mears

8. The police. The earliest souped-up cars were designed to help get illegal whiskey distributors away from the cops during Prohibition.

9. On the Staten Island side of the Verrazano-Narrows Bridge. All too many runners take the opportunity to urinate from the bridge.

10. Wilma Rudolph

Racing—All Kinds

Three Rolls — Answers

1. University of Oregon

2. Avenue des Champs-Élysées

3. Greta Waitz

4. Ironman Triathlon

5. Hambletonian Stakes

6. David Pearson

7. Six-Day Bicycle Races. One of the sport's biggest stars was New York Rangers hockey player Muzz Patrick.

8. Ultramarathons. Each year thousands of people push their bodies to the limit on all seven continents. Yes, even on Antarctica. Different races claim to be longer than all of the others. Some boast being a 3,000 mile race. Generally, runners will break down the long run by doing about 26 miles a day.

9. Mario Andretti

10. 3 minutes, 43.13 seconds in Rome. Though a fraction of a second slower, Noah Ngeny who finished second in that race, also broke the world record at the time. Both men ran about 16 seconds faster than Roger Bannister did in 1954 when he broke the 4 minute mile.

Personalities

 ## One Roll — Answers

1. Dennis Rodman

2. Rickey Henderson. He cashed the check after the Oakland A's asked him to. He was throwing off their bookkeeping.

3. Dave "The Hammer" Schultz

4. André the Giant

5. Lance Armstrong

6. Bob Knight

7. Carl Lewis. *TIME Magazine* ranked his performance as one of the Top 10 worst National Anthem renditions of all time. It is the only one on record that included an apology to a booing crowd, and a promise to improve as the song progressed.

8. Chi Chi Rodriguez

9. Roger Clemens

10. Evander Holyfield

Personalities

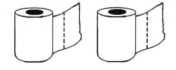 **Two Rolls — Answers**

1. Mike Eruzione

2. Pelé

3. Tony Hawk

4. Casey Stengel

5. Ty Cobb

6. Chris Evert

7. The Hanson Brothers

8. Arnold Palmer

9. Brandi Chastain

10. Babe Ruth

Personalities

Three Rolls — Answers

1. Diego Maradona

2. Renée Richards

3. Lee Trevino

4. Dick "Night Train" Lane

5. Cool Papa Bell

6. Reece "Goose" Tatum. Meadowlark Lemon would later take on the "clown prince" title for over 20 years with the Globetrotters.

7. Ilie Năstase

8. Billy Smith

9. Ray Nitschke

10. Steve "Psycho" Lyons. In 1990, after beating out a bunt for a hit, he pulled his pants down to wipe off the dirt. Lyons said that he forgot where he was. Unfortunately, he was in front of thousands of people at Tiger Stadium.

Famous Firsts

 ## One Roll — Answers

1. Goalie mask. Early in a game against the New York Rangers on November 1, 1959, Plante's nose was broken by an Andy Bathgate shot. He retired to the dressing room for repairs (there was no back-up goaltender on the bench in those days), and returned with the mask. His Montreal Canadiens won the game, 3-1. Previously, Plante had used the mask in practice, but never in a game.

2. Roger Clemens. He did it twice. First on April 29, 1986 vs. the Seattle Mariners. Second against the Detroit Tigers on Sept. 18, 1996. Kerry Wood struck out 20 Astros on May 6, 1998 at Wrigley Field.

3. The Triple Crown of Thoroughbred Racing

4. Babe Ruth

5. Lake Placid, New York

6. Wimbledon singles title

7. The Stanley Cup

8. The Houston Astros, who moved into the Astrodome in 1965

9. Tom Landry, from 1960-88. He won Super Bowl titles in 1972 and 1978.

10. O.J. Simpson, who was picked by the Buffalo Bills

Famous Firts

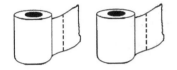

Two Rolls — Answers

1. Green Bay 35, Kansas City 10

2. Pete Rose hit safely in 44 consecutive games in 1978

3. Knute Rockne

4. The Boston Americans defeated the Pittsburgh Pirates 5 games to 3 in 1903

5. Hakeem Olajuwon. The Portland Trail Blazers never lived down taking Sam Bowie with the number two pick. In that same draft, Charles Barkley was drafted fifth by the Philadelphia 76ers, and John Stockton 16th by the Utah Jazz.

6. Larry Doby, for the Cleveland Indians in 1947, a few months after Jackie Robinson's debut with the Brooklyn Dodgers

7. Sonja Henie

8. World Series of Poker

9. Bobby Orr. He did it twice for the Boston Bruins: 1969-70 and 1974-75.

10. New York Mets in 1969

Famous Firsts

Three Rolls — Answers

1. Tom Dempsey of the New Orleans Saints booted a 63-yard bomb in 1970. But not without controversy! Dempsey was born without toes on his kicking foot, and wore a modified shoe with a larger surface around the toe region. Skeptics said that the shoe gave him an unfair advantage.

2. Gertrude Ederle in 1926

3. Bobby Carpenter for the Washington Capitals in 1984-85

4. Weed USA debuted their model in 1975, but response was disappointing. Prince had better luck with theirs the following year. If you said either, give yourself the points.

5. The New York Celtics were a barnstorming team that evolved into the "Original Celtics," who dominated in the 1920s

6. Willie O'Ree, who joined the Boston Bruins in 1957-58. Ironically it was the Boston Red Sox who were the *last* baseball team to integrate. They added Pumpsie Green in 1959.

7. William H. Taft in 1910

8. Indianapolis Racers of the defunct World Hockey Association in 1978. He played eight games for the team. He later starred for the Edmonton Oilers, Los Angeles Kings, St. Louis Blues, and New York Rangers.

9. Floyd Patterson

10. Cincinnati Reds at Crosley Field

Everything & Anything

 One Roll — Answers

1. Badminton

2. Superfecta

3. Manchester United

4. Eleven. Unless the score is tied at ten, in which someone would have to win by two. Competition used to go until 21, but that has been recently changed. If you still play to 21 in your basement, then give yourself the point.

5. Equestrian jumping or show jumping

6. Figure skating

7. Water polo

8. George Foreman. He was a two-time World Heavyweight Champion, and Olympic gold medalist. But if you don't know anything about boxing, he's the guy grilling pork-chops.

9. Setter

10. Orange

Everything & Anything

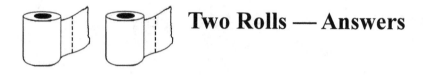

Two Rolls — Answers

1. Luge

2. Balance beam, floor, uneven bars, vault

3. Mogul skiing

4. Eleven

5. Gaelic football

6. Ken Shamrock

7. Matador

8. Synchronized swimming

9. Clean and jerk

10. Bocce

Everything & Anything

1. Curling. At one point in the 2010 Winter Games in Vancouver, more people were watching curling than anything else on television.

2. Coxswain. They coordinate commands and steer the boat.

3. Seven-ten split

4. Biathlon

5. Michigan Stadium, or "The Big House." The seating capacity is 109,901.

6. Equestrian vaulting, or voltige. It's popular in Central Europe, and has spread throughout the world. Competitors have to be careful not to get kicked on the dismount.

7. South Philadelphia Hebrew Association. The team was formed by Eddie Gottlieb, who later coached the Philadelphia Warriors in the NBA. Even in his 80s, Gottlieb annually created the entire NBA schedule by hand, even after the advent of computers.

8. Approximately ¾ inch thick

9. Max Schmeling. Just before World War II, this fight was about more than boxing. Schmeling represented Germany, while the "Brown Bomber" fought for the US. The fight lasted two minutes and four seconds.

10. Six. Three singles load the bases. The next three batted balls hit a runner. The runner is out and the batter is credited with a single each time.

Scorecard — Name: _____

Category	# Right		# of Pts.		Tot. Pts.
Football - 1 Roll		x	1	=	
Football - 2 Rolls		x	2	=	
Football - 3 Rolls		x	3	=	
Baseball - 1 Roll		x	1	=	
Baseball - 2 Rolls		x	2	=	
Baseball - 3 Rolls		x	3	=	
Basketball - 1 Roll		x	1	=	
Basketball - 2 Rolls		x	2	=	
Basketball - 3 Rolls		x	3	=	
Hockey - 1 Roll		x	1	=	
Hockey - 2 Rolls		x	2	=	
Hockey - 3 Rolls		x	3	=	
Golf & Tennis - 1 Roll		x	1	=	
Golf & Tennis - 2 Rolls		x	2	=	
Golf & Tennis - 3 Rolls		x	3	=	
Rules - 1 Roll		x	1	=	
Rules - 2 Rolls		x	2	=	
Rules - 3 Rolls		x	3	=	
Racing—All Kinds - 1 Roll		x	1	=	
Racing—All Kinds - 2 Rolls		x	2	=	
Racing—All Kinds - 3 Rolls		x	3	=	
Personalities - 1 Roll		x	1	=	
Personalities - 2 Rolls		x	2	=	
Personalities - 3 Rolls		x	3	=	
Famous Firsts - 1 Roll		x	1	=	
Famous Firsts - 2 Rolls		x	2	=	
Famous Firsts - 3 Rolls		x	3	=	
Everything & Anything - 1 Roll		x	1	=	
Everything & Anything - 2 Rolls		x	2	=	
Everything & Anything - 3 Rolls		x	3	=	

Grand Total

98

Scorecard — Name: _____

Category	# Right		# of Pts.		Tot. Pts.
Football - 1 Roll		x	1	=	
Football - 2 Rolls		x	2	=	
Football - 3 Rolls		x	3	=	
Baseball - 1 Roll		x	1	=	
Baseball - 2 Rolls		x	2	=	
Baseball - 3 Rolls		x	3	=	
Basketball - 1 Roll		x	1	=	
Basketball - 2 Rolls		x	2	=	
Basketball - 3 Rolls		x	3	=	
Hockey - 1 Roll		x	1	=	
Hockey - 2 Rolls		x	2	=	
Hockey - 3 Rolls		x	3	=	
Golf & Tennis - 1 Roll		x	1	=	
Golf & Tennis - 2 Rolls		x	2	=	
Golf & Tennis - 3 Rolls		x	3	=	
Rules - 1 Roll		x	1	=	
Rules - 2 Rolls		x	2	=	
Rules - 3 Rolls		x	3	=	
Racing—All Kinds - 1 Roll		x	1	=	
Racing—All Kinds - 2 Rolls		x	2	=	
Racing—All Kinds - 3 Rolls		x	3	=	
Personalities - 1 Roll		x	1	=	
Personalities - 2 Rolls		x	2	=	
Personalities - 3 Rolls		x	3	=	
Famous Firsts - 1 Roll		x	1	=	
Famous Firsts - 2 Rolls		x	2	=	
Famous Firsts - 3 Rolls		x	3	=	
Everything & Anything - 1 Roll		x	1	=	
Everything & Anything - 2 Rolls		x	2	=	
Everything & Anything - 3 Rolls		x	3	=	

Grand Total

Scorecard — Name: _____

Category	# Right		# of Pts.		Tot. Pts.
Football - 1 Roll		x	1	=	
Football - 2 Rolls		x	2	=	
Football - 3 Rolls		x	3	=	
Baseball - 1 Roll		x	1	=	
Baseball - 2 Rolls		x	2	=	
Baseball - 3 Rolls		x	3	=	
Basketball - 1 Roll		x	1	=	
Basketball - 2 Rolls		x	2	=	
Basketball - 3 Rolls		x	3	=	
Hockey - 1 Roll		x	1	=	
Hockey - 2 Rolls		x	2	=	
Hockey - 3 Rolls		x	3	=	
Golf & Tennis - 1 Roll		x	1	=	
Golf & Tennis - 2 Rolls		x	2	=	
Golf & Tennis - 3 Rolls		x	3	=	
Rules - 1 Roll		x	1	=	
Rules - 2 Rolls		x	2	=	
Rules - 3 Rolls		x	3	=	
Racing—All Kinds - 1 Roll		x	1	=	
Racing—All Kinds - 2 Rolls		x	2	=	
Racing—All Kinds - 3 Rolls		x	3	=	
Personalities - 1 Roll		x	1	=	
Personalities - 2 Rolls		x	2	=	
Personalities - 3 Rolls		x	3	=	
Famous Firsts - 1 Roll		x	1	=	
Famous Firsts - 2 Rolls		x	2	=	
Famous Firsts - 3 Rolls		x	3	=	
Everything & Anything - 1 Roll		x	1	=	
Everything & Anything - 2 Rolls		x	2	=	
Everything & Anything - 3 Rolls		x	3	=	

Grand Total

How did you do?

500 +   — King/Queen of the Throne

400-499 — Topper of the Hopper

350-399 — Porcelain Prince/Princess

300-349 — Toileterrific!

250-299 — Keep Flushing for the Stars

200-249 — Might Need a Plunger

150-199 — Gotta call the Plumber

Below 150 — Clogged

Try a different Toiletrivia Book!